IMMIGRANTS BUILD AMERICA

Latin American Immigrants

Hal Marcovitz

San Diego, CA

About the Author

Hal Marcovitz is a former newspaper reporter and columnist who has written more than two hundred books for young readers. He makes his home in Chalfont, Pennsylvania.

© 2025 ReferencePoint Press, Inc.
Printed in the United States

For more information, contact:
ReferencePoint Press, Inc.
PO Box 27779
San Diego, CA 92198
www.ReferencePointPress.com

ALL RIGHTS RESERVED.
No part of this work covered by the copyright hereon may be reproduced or used in any form or by any means—graphic, electronic, or mechanical, including photocopying, recording, taping, web distribution, or information storage retrieval systems—without the written permission of the publisher.

LIBRARY OF CONGRESS CATALOGING-IN-PUBLICATION DATA

Names: Marcovitz, Hal, author.
Title: Latin American immigrants / by Hal Marcovitz.
Description: San Diego, CA : ReferencePoint Press, Inc., [2025] | Series: Immigrants build America | Includes bibliographical references and index.
Identifiers: LCCN 2024003982 (print) | LCCN 2024003983 (ebook) | ISBN 9781678208400 (library binding) | ISBN 9781678208417 (ebook)
Subjects: LCSH: Hispanic Americans--Social conditions--Juvenile literature. | Immigrants--United States--Social conditions--Juvenile literature.
Classification: LCC E184.S75 M368 2025 (print) | LCC E184.S75 (ebook) | DDC 305.868/073--dc23/eng/20240212
LC record available at https://lccn.loc.gov/2024003982
LC ebook record available at https://lccn.loc.gov/2024003983

CONTENTS

Immigrants in the United States   4

Introduction   6
An Immigrant's Path to Stardom

Chapter One   9
Arrivals

Chapter Two   19
Getting Work

Chapter Three   28
Creating New Businesses

Chapter Four   37
Helping to Build Vibrant Communities

Chapter Five   46
Immigrants of Distinction

Source Notes   56
For Further Research   59
Index   61
Picture Credits   64

IMMIGRANTS IN THE UNITED STATES

Top Six Countries of Origin
- Mexico: 24%
- India: 6%
- China: 5%
- Philippines: 5%
- El Salvador: 3%
- Vietnam: 3%

US Immigrant Population
46.2 million, or 13.9% of total US population, in 2022

Earnings: Immigrant Workers and US-Born Workers

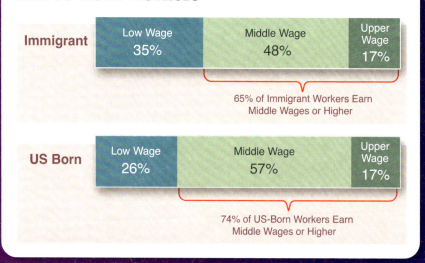

Immigrant — Low Wage 35% | Middle Wage 48% | Upper Wage 17%

65% of Immigrant Workers Earn Middle Wages or Higher

US Born — Low Wage 26% | Middle Wage 57% | Upper Wage 17%

74% of US-Born Workers Earn Middle Wages or Higher

Billion-Dollar Companies

Companies in the United States with at least one immigrant founder: 55%

Reasons for Immigrating to the United States

■ Major reason ■ Minor reason ■ Not a reason

Reason	Major	Minor	Not
For better economic and job opportunities	75%	13%	11%
For a better future for their children	68%	9%	20%
For better educational opportunities	62%	15%	21%
To have more rights and freedoms	50%	17%	29%
To join or accompany family members	42%	14%	41%
To get away from unsafe or violent conditions	31%	15%	51%

Starting Businesses

Immigrants are 80% more likely to start a business than people born in the United States.

Becoming Citizens

969,380 immigrants became naturalized US citizens in 2022.

INTRODUCTION

An Immigrant's Path to Stardom

Born in 1988, Ana de Armas grew up in the small, poverty-stricken Cuban community of Santa Cruz del Norte. Life on the island nation during de Armas's childhood in the 1990s and early 2000s could be a challenge: few people owned television (TV) sets, automobiles, or household appliances. Clothing was scarce—de Armas says she often wore clothes her older brother had outgrown. Food shortages were common. It was during her childhood, though, that de Armas first entertained dreams of becoming an actress.

De Armas knew she could never achieve her goal in Cuba. While still a teenager, she told her parents that she intended to leave Cuba and move to a country that would have the resources to help her develop her acting skills. "Before I even turned 18, I told my parents that was going to happen," she said in describing her plans to leave Cuba. "They've been so supportive, I was lucky. But it was me going into the unknown. I was just like, 'This is what I'm going to do with my life.' I put myself in their shoes and realize now what they were thinking, and how terrifying it must have been."[1]

The United States had the resources that would have helped de Armas realize her dream: university-level acting schools, professional theaters, and major studios that produce content for movies, TV networks, and streaming services. But during de Armas's teen years, the Cuban government maintained an icy relationship with the United States. Travel by Cuban citizens to the United States was prohibited.

Success and Stardom

Instead, de Armas elected to pursue her acting career in Spain, a nation to which the Cuban government did permit travel by its citizens. De Armas was near penniless when she arrived in Spain in 2007. Still, she soon landed a role on the TV series *El Internado* (in English, The Boarding School), a drama about the lives of young people from wealthy families attending a private school. De Armas quickly became a star, finding her talents in demand by Spanish TV and film producers. But she had even bigger plans: to star in films produced in Hollywood. She learned English and in 2016 made her first appearance in a Hollywood production—the comedy *War Dogs*. Today, de Armas lives in New York City and finds herself very much in demand by major film producers. In 2023, de Armas earned an Academy Award nomination for Best Actress for her role in *Blonde*, the tragic story of 1950s-era movie star Marilyn Monroe. In 2024, she was slated to star in the action-thriller *Ballerina*.

Although de Armas's route took her first to Spain, her ultimate goal was always to become a professional actress in America. As with many Latino immigrants, de Armas realized her home country could not provide her with the opportunities she needed to realize her dreams. Therefore, she looked to America, where she believed she could forge a new life. When de Armas and other Latino immigrants arrive in the United States, they find their talents very much in demand, helping to shape the economy and culture of their new homeland.

This photo shows Ana de Armas in the 2022 movie, Blonde. *De Armas immigrated to the United States from Cuba.*

7

Drive and Talent

This has been true for generations. Oscar de la Renta left the island nation of the Dominican Republic at the age of eighteen to study art in France. He arrived in New York City in 1963, soon establishing one of the world's top fashion design companies and setting a high bar for his competitors. Franklin Chang-Díaz was born on the island nation of Costa Rica and immigrated to the United States as a teen. He went on to earn a degree in engineering and in 1980 joined the National Aeronautics and Space Administration (NASA). Six years later he made the first of seven trips into space as an astronaut. During his tenure at NASA, Chang-Díaz headed a team that developed rocket engines used in NASA spacecraft. And many young people today are familiar with the work of actress Lilimar Hernandez—known to her fans as "Lilimar"—who was born in Venezuela and immigrated to the United States at the age of six.

Since arriving in the United States, she has appeared in numerous TV roles. On Instagram—where Lilimar has more than 1 million followers—she regularly posts her thoughts on current events, which she believes has a significant influence on how her young fans view the world. She says, "Every Saturday I (post about) a different topic, whether it's a controversial topic or a serious topic, or racial issues, or immigration. I wanted that to be there so people could see my opinion, and talk with me about it."[2]

> "Every Saturday I (post about) a different topic, whether it's a controversial topic or a serious topic, or racial issues, or immigration."[2]
>
> —Actress Lilimar Hernandez

Like de Armas, de la Renta, Chang-Díaz, and Lilimar, life in the United States has been the goal of millions of Latinos. And many have found success in the United States, reflecting the drive and talents that Latino immigrants have brought to their new homes in America. Through their work in industries ranging from high-tech innovators to factories that make consumer goods, and through businesses they have created and communities they have enriched or reinvigorated, Latin American immigrants have contributed to the fabric of life in America.

CHAPTER ONE

Arrivals

The work on the vast farm fields of Northern California was hard. The hours were long. The pay was low. And yet, Rigoberto Garcia Perez saw it as an opportunity. It allowed him to escape a life of poverty in Mexico for a new life in America, where he dreamed of owning a home and raising his children.

Garcia Perez grew up in Lalgodona, a small town in Mexico. His family owned a farm, but crop failures and the lack of water forced his father to sell most of the land. In 1958, at the age of twenty-four, Garcia Perez made the decision to come to America to find work on the farm fields of California.

His first trip across the border was made illegally. He hid aboard a freight train that crossed the border, jumped off the train in Los Angeles, and then made his way to Northern California, where he found work as a farm laborer picking cherries, strawberries, tomatoes, and other crops. After a few years in America, he returned home to get married but, again, found few opportunities to earn a living. Therefore, Garcia Perez traveled back to America—but this time, legally. He signed up to be a bracero, meaning "laborer" in Spanish. The Bracero Program dated back to World War II, when labor was desperately needed on American farm fields to feed the American people as well as the US troops battling overseas. Garcia Perez recalls the experience:

> We slept in big bunkhouses. It was like being in the army. One bed on top of another. Each person had their own bed, with a mattress, blanket and so on. Your soap, your razor. Everything in order. They'd tell us, "We want you

to keep this place clean. It's your house. When you get up, make your bed." And we all did it. We woke up when they sounded a horn or turned on the lights. We'd make our beds and go to the bathroom. Brush our teeth and whatever. We'd eat breakfast, and they'd give us our lunch. Some tacos or a couple of sandwiches, an apple and a soda. Sometimes they'd bring food to the field, and give us a meal there. It all depended. The camps were different. But we worked well.[3]

The Need for Work and Workers

Garcia Perez is among the millions of Mexicans and other Latinos (or Hispanics) who have made their way across the border into the United States in the past century. By the early 1900s, the United States had grown into a vibrant, industrialized society. Factories manufacturing all manner of consumer goods were rising in the American cities. Jobs were plentiful. South of the border, things were not as rosy. In 1910, a revolution was sparked in Mexico, leading to a decade of bloodshed, followed by many years of poverty and unrest. During this period many Mexicans fled their nation, heading north into the United States. Between 1910 and 1930, some six hundred thousand migrants from Mexico made their way to the United States, many crossing the border near the Texas city of El Paso—a name that, when translated into English, literally means "The Passage."

> "We slept in big bunkhouses. It was like being in the army. One bed on top of another."[3]
>
> —Former bracero Rigoberto Garcia Perez

Across America, many citizens, motivated largely by racial prejudice, rebelled against what is regarded by historians as the first wave of Latino immigration into the United States. But they were soon overruled by political leaders who, influenced by those industrialists in desperate need of workers, refused to adopt measures to slow the pace of Latino immigration. According to *New York Times* national editor Jia Lynn Yang, "Those favoring restriction—because

This photo, taken during the Mexican Revolution, shows people lying dead in the streets in Mexico City. Many Mexicans fled to the United States during the violent revolution.

they viewed Mexicans as racially inferior—did not prevail because of the growing clout of industry in America's West and employers' demand for Mexican labor."[4] In 1917, some anti-immigration political leaders were able to get a bill before Congress establishing literacy in English as a requirement for migrants to enter the United States; but the politically influential industrialists prevailed again, forcing Congress to grant exemptions for Latinos because their labor was sorely needed.

The need for Latino labor intensified in 1941 following America's entry into World War II, when millions of American men were drafted into the armed forces to fight in Europe and the South Pacific. The draft left many employers without sufficient workforces—a situation punctuated by the fact that the US government was now relying heavily on American industries and farms to provide weapons, vehicles, aircraft, ships, uniforms, boots, food, and everything else the military needed to carry out the war. Thus, the American government responded by establishing the Bracero

Program, enabling Mexicans to enter the country so they could work in those factories and farm fields, producing the goods and food vital not only to the war effort but also needed for the American people on the home front.

The Bracero Program

The Bracero Program was supposed to last for only as long as the war, which ended in 1945, but Congress left the law in place until 1964. In the years following the war, members of Congress were pressured by American agricultural barons to continue the Bracero Program because Mexican farm laborers were plentiful and their wages were low—some working for as little as three dollars a day. During the era of the Bracero Program, 4.5 million

This 1961 photo shows a Mexican migrant laborer who is employed under the Bracero Program harvesting tomatoes in Southern California. A large number of Latino immigrants came to the United States under the Bracero Program.

Guillermo del Toro's Path to Hollywood

Guillermo del Toro is one of the most successful film directors in Hollywood, winning three Academy Awards for Best Director. Among his films are the 2021 mystery *Nightmare Alley* and the 2019 science fiction thriller *The Shape of Water*.

Born in 1964 in Guadalajara, Mexico, del Toro had already carved out a successful career as a filmmaker in Mexico when he was offered opportunities to direct films in America. In 1997, he directed his first Hollywood production, the science fiction thriller *Mimic*. In 2019, del Toro was awarded a star on the Hollywood Walk of Fame: a plaque including his name and highlighting his accomplishments was laid into the concrete sidewalk along Hollywood Boulevard in Los Angeles, the city where he now makes his home.

Del Toro said achieving the honor illustrates the important role immigrants play in American society. "I can tell to all of you, all immigrants from every nation, that you should believe in the possibilities and not the obstacles," he stated. "Believe in the stories you have inside and believe that we all can make a difference and we all have stories to tell and we all can contribute to the art and the craft and the world in any way we see fit."

Quoted in BreAnna Bell, "Guillermo del Toro to Immigrants in America: 'Do Not Believe the Lies They Tell About Us,'" *Variety*, August 6, 2019. https://variety.com.

Mexicans found jobs in America, mostly on farm fields. After the program ended, historians have estimated that several hundred thousand Mexicans elected to remain in America rather than return home.

Garcia Perez was among the braceros who decided to stay in America. When the Bracero Program ended he applied for status as a legal immigrant and was granted permission to remain in the country. His wife and young children soon joined him. Eventually, Garcia Perez bought a home in the California city of Blythe. His children attended school in Blythe and went on to earn college degrees. "They have good jobs," Garcia Perez says of his children. "If they had gone to school in Mexico, they wouldn't have had the same chance. . . . I wanted a real future … and I found one."[5]

Garcia Perez's labors did more than just provide his family with a good home and opportunities for his children to receive quality educations. According to the US Department of Agriculture, starting in the 1960s—the era when many of the braceros elected to stay in America—the crop production on the nation's farms rose sharply. By the year 2000, crop production on American farms was more than double what it had been before Latino immigrants joined the agricultural labor force. Michele Cantos, editor of the publication *Hispanic Executive*, says "there is little argument that Latinos are the backbone of the industries feeding the nation—and the world, since US farmers export more than 20 percent of what they produce."[6]

Varied Circumstances

The decision by many braceros to remain in America marks the beginning of a wave of Latino immigration that continues to this day. In addition to Mexicans, migrants have traveled from the more than twenty Latin American countries seeking better lives in the United States. Since 1965, approximately 59 million immigrants have come to the United States from countries around the world. According to the Pew Research Center, close to half of these immigrants have come from Latin America. The reasons for coming are varied—and not unlike the reasons many other immigrants have come to the United States. Some have fled authoritarian regimes. Others have sought refuge from drug gangs and other violence. Still others hope that life in America will lead to jobs and opportunities they and their families did not have in their home countries.

> "For many Latinos, the United States offers a chance at a better life . . ."[7]
> —Pew Research Center

Life as an immigrant can be challenging. Learning a new language and customs, looking for work and a place to live, and sometimes encountering discrimination can complicate the transition from one country to another. Even so, many immigrants from Latin America prefer these challenges to those in their home countries. "For many Latinos," a 2021 Pew study found, "the United States offers a chance at a better life . . . A strong majority say the US provides more opportunities to get ahead . . . Majorities also say the US has better conditions for raising kids, access to health care and treatment of the poor."[7]

The Dreamers

Indeed, according to a US Census Bureau survey, in 2022 more than 15 million people born in Latin American countries were living on US soil. Among those immigrants are more than 10.7 million from Mexico, 1.4 million from El Salvador, 1.3 million from Cuba, 1.3 million from the Dominican Republic, and 1.1 million from Guatemala. A large number of those immigrants crossed the border into the United States illegally. Many of them have trekked through harsh and dangerous desert landscapes into Arizona, New Mexico, and Texas, eventually meeting up with friends and relatives who were already in the United States and willing to provide them with shelter and sustenance. According to US Customs and Border Protection, some 2.3 million Latinos were apprehended while attempting to make illegal border crossings into the United States in 2023. Moreover, the Pew Research Center

This 2000 picture shows a six-year-old girl who crossed into Arizona illegally from Mexico with family members. Young people who came across the border illegally with family and are now living as undocumented immigrants in the United States are often referred to as "Dreamers."

reports that an estimated 10.5 million Latinos who have made illegal border crossings over the past several decades are currently living in America—officially, they are known as undocumented immigrants.

Among the undocumented immigrants living in America are the so-called Dreamers—young people who accompanied their parents across the border and are now living in America. Typically, Dreamers have no memories of their former lives in Latino countries. They may have been carried across the border as infants or young children. Often, they do not learn they are in America illegally until reaching their teenage years. This typically happens when they apply for a driver's license or fill out college admission applications. These forms require Social Security numbers. Parents usually apply for this number when they provide information for their newborn's birth certificate. Since Dreamers were not born in the United States and are not US citizens, they do not have Social Security numbers.

In 2012 President Barack Obama created a program known as Deferred Action for Childhood Arrivals (DACA). DACA protects young people brought to America illegally by their parents from deportation while also providing them with many of the rights guaranteed to US citizens. It has enabled the Dreamers to remain in the United States, attend schools and colleges, and find employment without fear that they could be arrested and deported back to their home countries. According to the US Citizenship and Immigration Services, by the end of 2022 there were nearly 590,000 Dreamers living in America.

Protecting His Community

Many of the Dreamers have embraced the opportunities of living in the United States, becoming leaders in their communities and professions. Among them is Pedro Villalobos, who was born in the Mexican city of Cuernavaca and brought to America illegally by his parents when he was three years old. He grew up in Houston, Texas, where his father worked as a dishwasher in a restaurant

Latino Immigrants Are Vital to the US Economy

The Bracero Program illustrated how the American economy benefits from Latino immigration. In the decades since the program ended in the 1960s, studies have shown that Latino immigration remains vital to the health of the American economy.

A 2021 study by the Center for American Progress, a Washington, DC–based organization that studies economic and social issues, found that employers in the United States need far more workers than are currently available within the ranks of US citizens. This circumstance is particularly true in the health care field, which employs physicians, nurses, laboratory technicians, and similar professionals. The study found that granting legal status or citizenship to undocumented immigrants would, over the next decade, help create some four hundred thousand jobs and generate nearly $2 trillion in income for those workers. According to the report,

> Undocumented immigrants are critical to the nation's social infrastructure. . . . Across the country, they are building families and starting businesses, they are keeping hospitals open and functioning, and they are caring for Americans' loved ones. To that extent, legalization and a pathway to citizenship—which would raise wages for all workers [and] create hundreds of thousands of new jobs . . . is an investment in the country's infrastructure in and of itself.

Center for American Progress, "Citizenship for Undocumented Immigrants Would Boost US Economic Growth," June 14, 2021. www.americanprogress.org.

and his mother cleaned the tables. Eventually, Villalobos learned he was undocumented. In 2013, at the age of twenty-two, he was accepted into the DACA program.

Living with DACA protection, Villalobos earned a law degree and found a job as a prosecutor with the office of the district attorney (DA) for Travis County, Texas. In his job, Villalobos is tasked with prosecuting lawbreakers, often winning jail terms for defendants who have been charged with theft, assault, drug dealing, and similar crimes. In 2019, the Austin Bar Association—a professional organization of attorneys in Travis County—awarded Villalobos the Prosecutor Award for Excellence in Criminal Law. Travis County DA Margaret Moore asserts that "he's an impressive young man. At the DA's office, we look for trial strength and personality, people with good, balanced judgment. We don't emphasize seeking convictions, we emphasize seeking justice. Pedro fits the bill perfectly. He shines."[8]

Villalobos recalls that when he enrolled in law school, his original intent was to seek a career in immigration law—helping undocumented immigrants win legal status. But he found himself drawn to criminal law and the desire to help protect the citizens of his adopted homeland. Still a junior member of the Travis County DA staff, Villalobos aspires to one day tackle much more serious cases, such as homicides. He says, "As a prosecutor I want to grow to learn every aspect of criminal law. One day I hope I can do a murder trial. It's a natural progression. From a professional perspective, you have to be good at your job to take these cases. As a prosecutor you're going up against the best defense lawyers. I like going up against the best. I learn more from them than I do from my wins."[9]

> "As a prosecutor I want to grow to learn every aspect of criminal law. One day I hope I can do a murder trial. It's a natural progression."[9]
>
> —Travis County, Texas, prosecutor Pedro Villalobos

Villalobos's success illustrates how Dreamers—as well as other Latino immigrants—have contributed to American society. Despite the ordeals faced by many Latino immigrants—including the threat of arrest and deportation if they are undocumented—many of these immigrants have excelled and established themselves as important pillars of their new homeland.

CHAPTER TWO

Getting Work

Diana Barroso was a high school student in Colombia when her father lost his job. Because he was unable to find employment in his own country, the Barroso family moved to the United States. They made their new home in Cleveland, a city in southeast Tennessee. When Barroso started attending classes at the local high school, she encountered a major hurdle: she understood and spoke virtually no English.

Her family came together to help her. Barroso's aunt and uncle were already living in Cleveland and spoke English. Each evening, Barroso read articles out of the local newspaper to her uncle, who helped her understand words she did not know or could not pronounce. "Which was pretty much everything,"[10] Barroso recalls. Each night, the Barroso family watched only English-language movies and other programs on TV. At school, Barroso attended an English as a second language (ESL) class, which aided her familiarity with English as well. And she credits the vocal pop group Backstreet Boys with helping her improve her proficiency in English. Barroso was an avid fan and listened to the group's music daily. She found printouts of the lyrics to the group's songs and, wearing headphones, followed their voices as they pronounced the words on the pages before her. "I had a mad obsession with them back in the day," she says. "I would put on my headphones and try to match the lyrics . . . to what I was hearing."[11]

Within a year of moving to America, Barroso felt she had a good command of the English language. She went on to graduate from high school and then college. She found her first job with a social services agency in Cleveland, helping low-income pregnant women find prenatal care. Eventually, she found a job with a health insurance company, where her duties include communicating with Latino clients who do not speak English.

Jobs Throughout the Workforce

Barroso's drive and ambition are a reflection of the overall Latino immigrant community in the United States. According to the US Department of Labor, the unemployment rate in 2022 for foreign-born people living in America was 3.4 percent—slightly less than the overall unemployment rate of 3.7 percent reported that year for native-born Americans. And, according to the Labor Department, Latino immigrants account for nearly 50 percent of the foreign-born workforce in America. These statistics show how immigrants in general—and particularly Latino immigrants—are focused on finding work when they arrive in America.

Latino immigrants can be found throughout the workforce. As with Barroso, many Latino immigrants arrive while they are still young people and enroll in American schools. Many graduate from high school and go on to earn college diplomas, soon forging careers that enable them to buy homes and prosper on US soil. Indeed, according to the Pew Research Center, Barroso's experience is not uncommon among Latino immigrants. A 2018 report by the organization found that 26 percent of Latino immigrants earn college degrees in America. The percentage of all Americans who hold at least a bachelor's degree is just slightly higher at 31 percent, according to the US Census Bureau.

Out of necessity, many immigrants from Latin America, as well as other parts of the globe, are more focused on finding jobs than continuing their education. Many of these jobs involve manual labor. According to a study by the Migration Policy Institute, a Washington, DC–based organization that studies issues that face immigrants in America, about 28 percent of Latino immigrants find work as operators, fabricators, and laborers. These workers are employed in factories, where they operate machinery or toil on assembly lines; for trucking companies and railroads that ship

Latino immigrants are often young and typically enroll in American schools, going on to earn high school and college degrees.

freight; or in such jobs as digging trenches and laying asphalt for new roads. Although these types of jobs often involve hard, dirty, or repetitive tasks, they are nevertheless vital to the local and national economies.

Soon after arriving in America during the late 1980s from her home in Mexico, María Cambrón found work operating a sewing machine at a factory operated by Luvu Brands, a furniture manufacturer located in Doraville, Georgia. She believes sewing is a job she was born to do. "As a little girl I would sew dresses for my dolls," she says. "I made clothing for them. I've always liked sewing. I've been a seamstress for as long as I can remember."[12]

Jorge Ramírez works as a production manager at the same factory. He worked his way up to the position after he was hired for a job that required him to cut large pieces of sponge that are sewn into furniture cushions. In his experience, few

> "As a little girl I would sew dresses for my dolls. I made clothing for them. I've always liked sewing. I've been a seamstress for as long as I can remember."[12]
>
> —Textile worker María Cambrón

21

Latino Immigrants as Essential Workers

The COVID-19 pandemic illustrated the importance of essential workers. While millions of people worked remotely from home, many others were required to show up at their workplaces. Store clerks stocked supermarket shelves. Maintenance workers ensured that homes and commercial buildings had plumbing and electrical power. Farmworkers harvested crops so that people could eat.

According to a 2020 study by the Center for American Progress, during the pandemic as many as 5 million Latino immigrants—many of them undocumented—held jobs as essential workers. Tom Jawetz, vice president of the Center for American Progress, asserts,

> While the country has become increasingly aware of the essential work that immigrants—including undocumented immigrants—are doing during the pandemic, it is important to recognize this work didn't suddenly become essential during the pandemic, these people didn't suddenly start doing this work during the pandemic, and many of these jobs didn't suddenly become hazardous to the health and safety of workers during the pandemic. This is work and these are workers who have long been essential to the functioning of this country and its economy, and frequently they have done this work—often at significant personal risk—with far too little recognition or reward.

Quoted in Center for American Progress, "Immigrants as Essential Workers During COVID-19," September 28, 2020. www.americanprogress.org.

---

native-born Americans seem to have an interest in fashioning textiles—clothing, bed linens, furniture covers, tablecloths, and numerous other products. And so, lacking a labor pool of skilled textile workers, many American companies contract with textile factories in Asia—particularly in China—to make the goods that are sold in America. He says, "Sewing is becoming obsolete here in the United States, because many things are being produced in China."[13] Ramírez believes that Latinos skilled in sewing are vital to the success of the American textile industry.

From Dishwasher to Server

Cambrón's success illustrates how many Latino immigrants are able to use the skills they learned in their home countries to help them find jobs in America. However, many Latino immigrants arrive in America with few skills that US employers would find useful. As such, they must learn new skills. In many cases, they are drawn to the service sector of employment. Service sector jobs include restaurant workers, store clerks, janitors, landscapers, and similar positions. According to the Migration Policy Institute, about 26 percent of Latino immigrants find employment in the US service sector.

Such jobs as cleaning floors in school buildings and stocking shelves in supermarkets require a knack, but those skills are often acquired on the job—a fact learned by twenty-one-year-old Aquiles Sanchez. Soon after arriving in America from El Salvador with his parents and siblings, Sanchez found a job as a dishwasher in a restaurant in West New York, New Jersey. It is a low-paying job: dishwashers generally make minimum wage, which is the lowest salary an employer is legally required to pay under the laws of the states in which they do business. In many states, the minimum wage is $7.25 an hour, or roughly $15,000 a year.

But Sanchez worked hard and soon found himself promoted to busboy. Busboys report to tables where diners have finished

Many Hispanic immigrants are drawn to the service sector of employment. Service sector jobs include restaurant workers, store clerks, janitors, landscapers, and similar positions.

their meals, collecting the used plates and utensils—again, a low-paying job but still a promotion. Within a short time, Sanchez was promoted again, this time to food runner; this job requires him to carry the fresh meals from the restaurant kitchen to the customers in the dining room. Sanchez believes he is on a path to become a server, which pays much better than dishwasher, busboy, and food runner. Servers greet diners, take their orders, and are largely responsible for ensuring the diners are treated respectfully and enjoy their meals. According to the Labor Department, most restaurant servers earn about $30,000 a year.

> "I really like the US, this is a country of opportunity, of people who want to keep fighting and get ahead."[14]
>
> —Restaurant worker Aquiles Sanchez

In Sanchez's case, when he started work as a dishwasher, he earned about $400 a month. Now, as a food runner, he earns about $400 a week, or about $21,000 a year. As a server, Sanchez believes he can earn a salary that will enable him to find a home of his own, marry, and start a family. "I am grateful they have given me the opportunity to keep advancing," Sanchez says of his employer. "I really like the US, this is a country of opportunity, of people who want to keep fighting and get ahead."[14]

The Plight of Many Latinas

Although workers such as Sanchez, Cambrón, and Barroso have found jobs they enjoy that enable them to earn decent wages, many Latino immigrants have found fewer opportunities available to them. This is particularly true for Latino women—Latinas—many of whom find themselves working for years in the low-paying job of housekeeper.

Housekeeping is a common job in the United States. Hotels employ housekeepers—often known as maids—to clean guest rooms, change bed linens, vacuum hallways, empty trash cans, and so on. In the typical American office, after the sales staff members, information technology workers, and executives leave

The Future for Latino STEM Workers

The US economy has a seemingly unending need for STEM workers—those skilled in science, technology, engineering, and mathematics. According to the US Bureau of Labor Statistics, 11 million workers in the United States will be employed in STEM fields by 2031; however, by then there will still be a shortage of some 1 million STEM workers. A study by the Washington, DC–based American Immigration Council reported that some 120,000 immigrants from Mexico held STEM jobs in the United States during 2022. According to the statistics, STEM workers born in Mexico compose about 5 percent of all foreign-born STEM workers in the United States.

Labor industry experts believe young Latino immigrants will be instrumental in making up the shortfall of STEM workers in the future. Chris Wilkie, chief executive officer of the Society of Hispanic Professional Engineers, says, "When you look at that demographic growth and you look at the job growth in STEM, it makes sense [to conclude] that the Hispanic community will be not only a large part of that solution, but likely *the* solution."

Quoted in Kayla Young, "STEM Jobs are Growing—and Latinos Could Be Key to Filling Them," WFAE-FM, October 28, 2022. www.wfae.org.

---

for the day, the housekeeping crew shows up at night to clean the office. Many homeowners too busy to clean their own homes also hire housekeepers. The housekeepers come into their homes once a week or so to clean bathrooms, vacuum carpets, polish kitchen floors, and dust furniture.

Housekeepers generally earn no more than minimum wage. According to the Labor Department, the job of housekeeper typically pays about $15,000 a year. Moreover, that salary is for a full-time housekeeper. Many Latinas find themselves working in part-time jobs because they also care for young children and, therefore, are unable to leave their homes for full-time employment. According to UnidosUS, a Washington, DC–based group that aids low-income Latino immigrants, some 46 percent of women who immigrated to the United States from Latin America work as housekeepers, meaning millions of Latinas must find a way to survive in the United States while earning very low wages.

Among those low-paid workers is Miriam Paredo Roque, who immigrated to the United States in 2007 from her home in Veracruz, Mexico. Since arriving in Los Angeles, Paredo Roque has found work as a housekeeper. She typically earns just $10,000 a year to support herself and her son. Still, she perseveres. "I've been able to save as much as I can, to not live paycheck to paycheck,"[15] she says.

A Comfortable Life

Among millions of immigrants from Latin America are many who have forged successful careers at home. When they arrive in America, they bring with them the expertise and skills that enabled them to prosper. Ana Palmira Almanzar was thirty-seven years old when she arrived in America in 1992, emigrating from the Dominican Republic. Although the Dominican Republic suffers from widespread poverty, Almanzar and her family members lived a prosperous life there. Almanzar's mother worked at a bank. Her father was the manager of a laboratory that manufactured prescription drugs. They elected to emigrate when one of Almanzar's sisters moved to America. Wishing to keep the family together, Almanzar and her parents followed her sister to America, making their homes in Miami. However, Almanzar notes that family members had also grown wary of living in the Dominican Republic due to a rising crime rate in the country. "The Dominican Republic is a pretty country, but we thought there was more crime and *delincuencia* (delinquency),"[16] she says.

After arriving in America, Almanzar found work in real estate, selling homes and commercial properties. She was very successful, and for several years her annual salary reached $140,000. But in America, the real estate market is very much dependent on a healthy economy. In times when unemployment rises and wages do not keep up with the cost of living, people are generally less likely to buy new homes. Late in the first decade of the 2000s, the American economy was hit with a downturn and, as a result, Almanzar's work in real estate dropped off. To supplement her income, she found a part-time job selling women's cosmetics at a

> "I've been able to save as much as I can, to not live paycheck to paycheck."[15]
>
> —Housekeeper Miriam Paredo Roque

A housekeeper works in a South Carolina hotel. Latinas often take housekeeping jobs in the United States, where they usually earn no more than minimum wage.

Miami department store. She still sells real estate but has not yet come close to matching her income in her more prosperous years.

But Almanzar says she is very comfortable with the life she leads in America and the earning opportunities she has found. "I see myself as middle class. When there's not much left over after paying the bills, that's middle class," she laughs. "There's always room here, and possibilities."[17]

Almanzar and the other Latino immigrants reflect a spirit found in their community—they want to work and succeed and believe America offers them the best opportunity to achieve their goals. Thus, when they arrive, they may find themselves climbing the promotion ladder in a local restaurant, selling real estate and lipstick, helping other Latinos find health care, or doing a job—such as sewing—that is otherwise becoming a forgotten skill in America. And in so doing, they not only forge paths to success for themselves but help provide the foundation on which the American economy is built.

CHAPTER THREE

Creating New Businesses

Growing up in Colombia, Maria Artunduaga aspired to be a physician. After graduating from medical school in her native country, Artunduaga moved to the United States in 2007. Initially, she was drawn to the practice of cosmetic surgery. What appealed to her most was the ability to improve the lives of patients who have been disfigured in accidents or from birth. In order to practice medicine in the United States, however, she first had to gain accreditation. She attended Harvard Medical School and then transferred to the University of Chicago.

It was during this time that she learned of her grandmother's declining health. As a young child, Artunduaga watched her grandmother struggle with the debilitating disease chronic obstructive pulmonary disease, known more familiarly as COPD. The condition causes the pathways in the human body that provide air to the lungs to narrow, making it difficult for COPD patients to breathe. People who suffer from COPD often need to wear devices, which include tubes that snake into their noses, to help pump air into their lungs. They may also need to rely on prescription medications. Moreover, the disease usually gets worse as time goes by. According to the National Institutes of Health, nearly 16 million Americans suffer from COPD.

Eventually, COPD took the life of Artunduaga's grandmother. So, after completing her cosmetic surgery studies and achieving accreditation in the field, Artunduaga elected instead to pursue a new path in medicine: helping COPD patients cope with their conditions and improve their quality of life. She recalls her decision to step away from a career in cosmetic surgery: "Probably because I have a very surgeon-like mentality, and I like solutions that are quick, I just decided to leave everything. I was like, 'It's now or never.'"[18]

Sylvee

Artunduaga believes that most COPD patients do not realize their conditions are worsening and, therefore, may not seek assistance from their physicians until it is too late. To help improve the lives of COPD patients, Artunduaga enrolled in the University of California, Berkeley, where she received a degree in engineering. Using her skills as a physician and engineer, Artunduaga sought to develop a device she planned to name "Sylvee" in tribute to her grandmother, whose name was Sylvia.

The device attaches to the chest and can detect sounds within the lungs that indicate changes in the level of COPD symptoms. Patients can then alert their physicians of the changes. Physicians can then take appropriate steps, such as altering their patients' prescriptions, changing the levels of air pressure pumped into their lungs, or even ordering hospitalization.

Artunduaga credits her student years in Colombia for helping her develop the technology behind Sylvee. Medical students, as well as other young people in Colombia, have few technological resources to assist in their training, she says, making them more reliant on their own instincts and personal drive. As she conceived her ideas for better detecting the worsening symptoms of COPD, Artunduaga wondered whether the sounds within a COPD patient's lungs could be picked up by a compact device. "I'm very good at finding connections amongst unexpected things," says Artunduaga. "I'm a good diagnostician. In Colombia we don't have a lot of technologies that are available here in the States, so we're very good at using our heads to diagnose something. That's sort of my superpower."[19]

> "I'm very good at finding connections amongst unexpected things. I'm a good diagnostician."[19]
>
> —Physician and engineer Maria Artunduaga

Some immigrants were doctors in their countries of origin. In order to practice medicine in the United States, however, they usually have to repeat at least some of their education to gain accreditation.

To produce Sylvee, in 2018 Artunduaga founded a company she named Samay Health, headquartered in Mountain View, California. The name is drawn from the word for "deep breath" in Quechua, a language spoken by Indigenous peoples in Latin America. By 2024, Samay employed nearly two dozen engineers, physicians, software designers, and other staff members. Sylvee was not yet available to patients. In the United States, all medical devices and prescription drugs must undergo a lengthy review by the US Food and Drug Administration (FDA). But Artunduaga predicted Sylvee would soon receive full FDA approval and be made available to COPD patients in the United States and elsewhere, vastly improving, and lengthening, the lives of COPD patients.

Venezuelan Specialties from a Food Truck

Artunduaga is one of many immigrants from Latin America who have gone on to establish their own businesses. According to a

2023 study by researchers at Stanford University in California, some 17 percent of all US businesses are owned by Latin American immigrants. Moreover, the Stanford study reported that those businesses earn some $18 trillion a year—about 8 percent of all profits earned by businesses in America. The Stanford study predicts that businesses owned by Latin American immigrants will make up 29 percent of all US businesses by 2050.

Not all of these businesses involve technologically sophisticated products on the scale of Samay. Many businesses established by Latino immigrants are quite small—similar to the business founded by Venezuelan native Miguel Angel Navarro Castillo. Castillo, born in 1984, had worked as a journalist under two authoritarian presidents. As part of his job, he had reported on government corruption. In 2016, Castillo says, he was driving along a street in the Venezuelan capital, Caracas, when he was suddenly ordered by police to stop his car. He recalls, "Seven motorcyclists circled my car . . . rifles pointed at me."[20]

The Business of Caring for Pets

Pet owners who travel frequently turn to pet-sitting services. For a fee, a pet sitter comes into the home to look after the dog or cat. Some pet-sitting businesses provide locations—typically storefronts—where people drop off their pets and the animals stay for the duration of their owners' travels.

Yessy Feliz, an immigrant from the Dominican Republic, decided this was the business for her. Her love for dogs and cats as well as her desire to open her own business led her to establish Tails Boston in 2012. Her business cares for pets while their owners are traveling. Within five years of its founding, Tails Boston became so popular that Feliz expanded the business to two locations, employing twenty-two people who work in those locations but also travel across the city to care for pets in their owners' homes. Feliz says her goal is to make her clients' pets as comfortable as possible. For example, dog owners are required to fill out extensive questionnaires describing the habits and personalities of their animals. "We take into account how dogs will react in a group environment," Feliz says. "If dogs are anxious or overwhelmed, we do not put them together."

Quoted in Lauren Bennett, "Tails Boston Ready to Become Part of Your Dog or Cat's Family," *Jamaica Plain Gazette*, June 29, 2022. https://jamaicaplaingazette.com.

Castillo was taken into custody by the police. "They questioned me . . . and threatened my life,"[21] he says. Castillo was released from custody, but fearing for his life, he knew he had to leave Venezuela. In 2016 he fled to the United States, arriving in North Carolina with just forty-five dollars in his pocket.

Castillo initially found work as a dishwasher in a restaurant. He worked hard, lived frugally, and saved his earnings until he had enough money to open his own business—a food truck—in 2018. His truck travels along the streets of Surf City, a coastal town in North Carolina whose beaches are popular among tourists. His truck ambles along the streets that border the city's beaches, selling food to beachgoers. His truck may show up at public events in Surf City—for example, a 5-kilometer run where participants and spectators line up at his truck for lunch.

Castillo sells Venezuelan food. Many of his customers enjoy his arepas, which consist of chicken, beef, or vegetables wrapped in warm buns made from cassava flour. The cassava is a sweet, nutty vegetable that grows mostly in South America. Castillo says, "I really appreciate the people, and I have pride for

Many Latin American immigrants establish their own businesses, including food trucks. This is because cooking is a skill they have learned in their home country, so this type of business comes naturally to them.

my family and me. I send the people [of Surf City] good vibrations. I need the people to have a little taste of Venezuela!"[22]

One New Business Leads to Another

Most new businesses established in America—including those created by Latino immigrants—are likely to start out as small enterprises. But some small businesses grow into larger companies.

Carlos Castro was twenty-five years old when he immigrated to the United States from El Salvador in the early 1980s. A civil war had broken out in the country. Castro was a college student at the time, attending classes at a school in San Salvador, the nation's capital. Street fighting was often fierce in San Salvador's neighborhoods, and Castro felt his life was in danger. "The situation started to become violent, and [anti-government guerrilla fighters] got weapons," Castro says. "The city that I was raised in was overrun by the guerrillas twice, and then the soldiers came to confront them. In one of these conflicts, I was feeling the bullets flying over my head."[23]

> "I send the people [of Surf City] good vibrations. I need the people to have a little taste of Venezuela!"[22]
>
> —Food truck owner Miguel Angel Navarro Castillo

Thus, Castro left El Salvador. Traveling first to Los Angeles, he eventually settled in Washington, DC. For the next few years, he held many low-paying jobs, mostly working in restaurants as well as in construction jobs. As a construction worker, his creativity in solving problems on the job impressed his boss, who started referring small jobs to Castro. These small jobs led to Castro starting his own business. Castro explains,

> This is how I started my construction company. I got my business license and I had a few customers. Because I was just starting in the business, I did not charge a lot. So, people would see that I do a good job without asking for a lot of money. One person recommended me to the other so this is how I expanded my customer list. I had this construction company for four years.[24]

While running his construction business, Castro hatched an idea to open a grocery store to specifically serve the needs of Latino customers. Castro believes Latinos living in the United States often have difficulty finding the types of foods—and their ingredients—that are commonly consumed in their home countries. In 1990, Castro opened Todos Supermarket in Woodridge, Virginia, a community 55 miles (about 88 km) south of Washington, DC.

Castro devoted a lot of his time to the success of his supermarket—so much, in fact, that he found himself neglecting his construction business. Eventually, Castro elected to close the construction business and focus all his time and energy on Todos.

Castro's dedication paid off. He has since opened a second Todos in Woodridge, employing more than 180 workers at both stores. Among the features offered by Todos are free rides home for customers who purchase more than seventy-five dollars in groceries; advertising and signage around the stores in both English and Spanish; accounting services for customers who need help

This photo shows a Hispanic market in Brooklyn, New York. Grocery stores are just one type of new business established by Latino immigrants.

The Birth of Zumba

Many people take Zumba classes as a way to stay fit. Zumba exercises are aerobic in nature, meaning they are fast-paced and require students to constantly move their bodies to keep in step. In doing so, they burn calories and help build up strength in their hearts, lungs, and limbs. And when students exercise the Zumba way, they are doing it to the timing of zesty Latino music.

Zumba Fitness was founded in 1986 by Beto Perez, an immigrant and onetime aerobics instructor from Colombia. His business, based in Hallendale Beach, Florida, has enjoyed widespread popularity. By 2023, some 15 million students were enrolled in weekly classes at 110,000 gyms in 125 countries authorized to teach Zumba.

Perez's company does not own the gyms—rather, it licenses the use of its exercises and music to instructors trained by the company. Some of these instructors have started their own Zumba classes and become entrepreneurs themselves. "We're helping the instructors to become entrepreneurs and make a living out of it," says Alberto Aghion, president and chief operating officer of Zumba Fitness, who also emigrated from Colombia and cofounded the company with Perez.

Quoted in Cammy Clark, "Zumba's Latin Rhythms on the Move in the Fitness World," *Seattle Times*, February 20, 2012. www.seattletimes.com.

---

preparing their US tax returns, and translators who help customers understand English-language documents they may need to review.

Castro says it took plenty of hard work to build Todos into what it is today. But transitioning from what had been a successful, albeit small, construction business into an enterprise that requires thousands of square feet in commercial real estate space and employs nearly two hundred workers also involved some risk-taking. He recalls,

> First, I had to take the risk as many entrepreneurs do. I took the risk because I was thinking that since I had nothing when I was growing up, going back to nothing did not really scare me. I know that I could start all over again. So, courage plays a very important role for success. When you are an entrepreneur, you are willing to risk a lot. Another factor that facilitated the success of the grocery business was the fact that I was always involved with the community here. For instance, in some Latin American countries if you

are a business owner, people look at you as someone who knows a lot or is wise, so we had that going on here, too. I was trying to help people from day one. They would ask me all different kinds of questions: if I know a lawyer for a divorce, immigration law-related questions, but also little things such as translating letters from English to Spanish for the newcomers.[25]

> "First, I had to take the risk as many entrepreneurs do. I took the risk because I was thinking that since I had nothing when I was growing up, going back to nothing did not really scare me."[25]
>
> —Todos Supermarket owner Carlos Castro

The journeys taken by Castro, Castillo, and Artunduaga illustrate the entrepreneurial spirit harbored by many Latino immigrants. After they arrived in America, they knew they possessed the skills to not only earn their livings but to build businesses as well. Whether they sell groceries to consumers, sandwiches to beachgoers, or are developing new technologies to improve the lives of COPD patients, these entrepreneurs have found ways to become steadfast contributors to the US economy.

CHAPTER FOUR

Helping to Build Vibrant Communities

The small city of Reading, Pennsylvania, can be found in the heart of what for centuries has been the home of the Pennsylvania Dutch. Members of the Pennsylvania Dutch community are the descendants of immigrants from Germany and neighboring nations who began arriving in America during the early years of the seventeenth century.

After arriving in America, these immigrants continued to speak German and maintained the lifestyles they knew in Europe. Even today, visitors to the region may hear longtime residents speaking with German accents and occasionally see members of the Amish community—Pennsylvania Dutch citizens who eschew modern conveniences and can be seen ambling along the road in horse-drawn carriages.

Many of the Pennsylvania Dutch immigrants were farmers. Over the centuries, the fields surrounding the city of Reading were largely devoted to growing mushrooms. In the latter half of the twentieth century, word spread throughout the Latino immigrant community that jobs were available on Pennsylvania Dutch farms. Immigrants from Mexico and the Dominican Republic flocked to Reading. Many farmworkers also came from Puerto Rico—the American territory in the Caribbean where Spanish is the native language.

Today, Reading has a large, bustling, and diverse community of Latinos. In fact, the 2020 US Census found that Latinos now make up the majority of Reading's population. Sixty-nine percent of Reading residents have roots in Latin American countries. It is now more common to hear Spanish accents on the city's streets than it is to hear Pennsylvania Dutch accents.

Moreover, the city of Reading can certainly be regarded as a component of the "Rust Belt," which is the older Eastern and Midwestern US cities where factories have closed, leading to a downward trend in population as citizens leave for opportunities elsewhere. However, that downward spiral has not occurred in Reading, where the city's population has grown since the 2010 US Census. The current population is about ninety thousand—some seven thousand more residents than were counted in 2010.

Secondary Migration

Although mushroom farming is still very much a part of the economy of Reading, most Latino immigrants who now make Reading their home are not farmworkers. Rather, they are service workers, business owners, teachers, lawyers, physicians, and members of other professions. In many cases, Reading was not the city where they found their first homes in America. For example, many members of the Dominican Republic community in Reading originally immigrated to New York City, which itself has a large community of migrants from the Caribbean island nation.

But the cost of living in New York City is very high, which is typical of big cities. Everything from rents to groceries to utilities such as electricity and water typically cost more in big cities than in smaller towns. Finding the high cost of living too much to bear, many Latino immigrants eventually look for homes in smaller communities. (Sociologists call this trend "secondary migration"—finding new homes in other cities after first establishing their homes in the cities of their arrival in America.) In the case of many immigrants from the Dominican Republic, their interests were drawn to Reading.

This photo shows a man working at a mushroom farm near Reading, Pennsylvania. Many Latinos immigrated to this area in the latter half of the twentieth century to work on farms.

Born in the Dominican Republic, Gregorio Zarzuela's path led him first to New York City. He found work in factories and restaurants but wanted to own a business—a small grocery store known as a bodega. In fact, he did buy a bodega in New York City but was forced to sell the store after a couple of years. The costs of running the store—stocking it with groceries, paying utility bills—were simply too high for Zarzuela to maintain a profitable business.

Zarzuela was aware that other immigrants from the Dominican Republic had moved to Reading. He made inquiries about the city and reached the decision to move there. Zarzuela bought a home in Reading in 2004. Soon after moving to the city, he opened a bodega. "Living in Reading is just too good," he stated in a 2006 interview. "Business is slow, but [in Reading] you can live from it. Here I open at 7:30 a.m., and at 6:30 I head home to have a barbecue or make dinner. In New York, it was 6 a.m. to midnight. I love New York, but I can't go back."[26]

> "Living in Reading is just too good. Business is slow, but [in Reading] you can live from it."[26]
>
> —Reading, Pennsylvania, bodega owner Gregorio Zarzuela

Big Cities Benefit from Immigrant Homebuyers

Small cities like Reading, Pennsylvania, have been revived by Latino immigrants, but much larger cities have also benefited from the same trend. Chicago is a typical example. Starting in the 1960s, Chicago—one of America's largest cities—saw its population start to decline as residents fled to the suburbs. By the 1990s, Chicago's population was reported at 2.7 million people, or some 760,000 residents smaller than it had been in 1960.

One of the Chicago neighborhoods hit hard by the population decline was South Lawn, where vacant homes and apartment buildings lined street after street. Richard Dolejs, an immigrant from Mexico and community activist who established a real estate sales business in South Lawn, recognized the trend. He persuaded local banks to write mortgages—bank loans that enable borrowers to buy homes—for newly arrived Latino immigrants. Dolejs recalls his conversations with local bankers: "We said: 'Well, what about the Mexican community? We should apply to that group and try to bring them in.'" These actions helped those immigrants buy homes in South Lawn and other Chicago neighborhoods.

With time, Chicago's population has stabilized. In 2020, the city's population was recorded at virtually the same as its population in 1990.

Quoted in A.K. Sandoval-Strausz, "How Latinos Saved American Cities," *Washington Post*, November 8, 2019. www.washingtonpost.com.

Today, the cityscape of Reading reflects the interests of the Latino population. Residents can shop at the Bravo Supermarket in town, where they can find groceries favored by Latino households. Many Latino households celebrate what is known as the "quinceañera"—the fifteenth birthday of a daughter, marking her passage into womanhood. The celebrations are formal, meaning the celebrant and her Latina girlfriends wear gowns. Many clothing stores in Reading sell gowns for the quinceañera. And there also are dozens of Latino restaurants in the city.

Saving the Cities

Reading is a small city, but it is reflective of a significant trend that has occurred within many cities. For decades, the populations of many American cities had been declining. This was due mostly to the desire of city residents to move to suburban communities.

This trend led to many vacant apartment buildings, row houses, and other residences found in cities. And with fewer customers populating cities and fewer employees available to work for local retailers and manufacturers, many large and small businesses left the cities as well.

Starting in the 1990s, however, city populations started growing again. A.K. Sandoval-Strausz, a professor of history at Pennsylvania State University, explains that "the cities of the United States began a long decline after about 1950. That was the peak population for pretty much all industrial cities. . . . By the 1970s and 1980s, it looked like the big American city had simply come and gone."[27]

According to Sandoval-Strausz, Latino immigrants are primarily responsible for the rebirth of many American cities. They have provided students for public schools where enrollment had declined. They have started new businesses that provide employment for city residents. They pay local taxes, enabling their city governments to fix streets, maintain utilities, and provide police for the protection of the citizens. "They begin to repopulate schools and churches, they save housing markets," says Sandoval-Strausz. "They did things, without which the great urban recovery could not have happened. We're talking about home construction, building maintenance, child care, food service and groundskeeping. These are all very Latino- and Latina-heavy industries."[28]

> "[Latinos] begin to repopulate schools and churches, they save housing markets. They did things, without which the great urban recovery could not have happened."[28]
>
> —Pennsylvania State University history professor A.K. Sandoval-Strausz

Little Havana

Despite the high cost of living in big cities like New York, many Latinos do choose to stay. For example, the population of Miami has increased since 1990, when the number of city residents was recorded at about 359,000. The 2020 US Census reported Miami's population at about 442,000 residents. Moreover,

> "I would prefer to die to reach my dream and help my family. The situation in Cuba is not very good."[29]
>
> —Cuban immigrant Jeiler del Toro Diaz

in Miami, Latinos are in the majority. More than 305,000 of the city's residents—about 69 percent—have roots in Latin American countries.

A majority of the Latinos living in Miami emigrated from Cuba or are the descendants of parents and grandparents who left the island. It is easy to see why Cubans have migrated to Miami. In escaping Cuba's poverty and repressive government, most migrants land first in Florida. There, they soon connect with relatives and friends already living in Miami. "I would prefer to die to reach my dream and help my family. The situation in Cuba is not very good,"[29] Cuban migrant Jeiler del Toro Diaz said shortly after he and other migrants reached a Florida beach in a rickety boat in 2023.

As the center of Cuban immigration in America, Miami has grown to reflect the culture of the Caribbean island. In fact, there

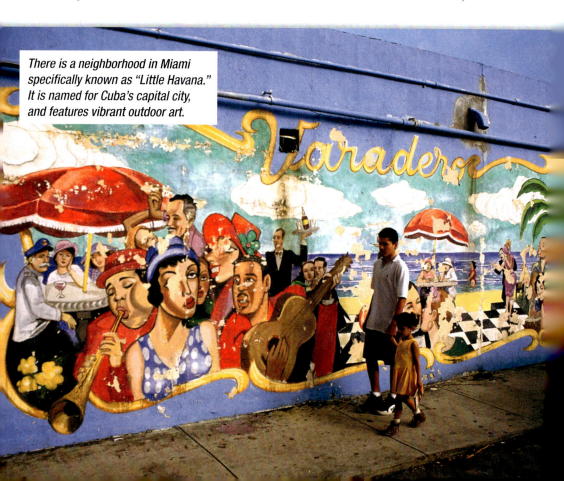

There is a neighborhood in Miami specifically known as "Little Havana." It is named for Cuba's capital city, and features vibrant outdoor art.

The Oil Fields of North Dakota

Visit Watford City, North Dakota, and you may encounter such restaurants as the Tomate Mexican Grill or Tacos La Mexicana. In the past decade, Watford City's immigrant population has seen dramatic growth. North Dakota—with its long winters and barren plains—is nothing like the tropical climates and forests found throughout Latin America. Nevertheless, Latino immigrants have flocked to North Dakota because of the abundance of jobs available in the state's oil fields. According to the US Census Bureau, in 2010 McKenzie County, which includes Watford City, reported virtually no Latino residents. In 2022, the Census Bureau reported the county is home to some seventeen hundred Latinos—or about 12 percent of the county's total population of about fourteen thousand residents.

It is a trend recognized by the state government, which has adopted measures to help build more homes in Watford City while also providing local schools with larger budgets to accommodate the needs of migrants and to help keep the town a vibrant and growing community. Born in Mexico, Yolanda Rojas and her family immigrated to Watford City. She says "It's my home. I love it. Here I discovered a beauty. It's a peaceful place. It's very safe. It's a great environment to raise a family."

Quoted in Reynaldo Leaños Jr., "Ever Since the Oil: Part Two," Latino USA, October. 21, 2022. www.latinorebels.com.

---

is a neighborhood in Miami specifically known as "Little Havana." It is named for Cuba's capital city. The hotel-booking website Generator reports, "Just west of downtown Miami sits Little Havana; a vibrant riverside neighborhood known the world over for its colorful streets, family-run businesses, authentic restaurants and thriving arts scene. And though you'll find traces of Cuban culture wherever you are in Miami, Little Havana is the beating heart of it all."[30]

Throughout Little Havana, visitors will find restaurants specializing in Cuban cuisine, art galleries and museums featuring works by Cuban artists and craftspeople, and the Calle Ocho ("Eighth Street") Walk of Fame. The destination, which features outdoor art and murals as well as pink stars embedded in the sidewalks, celebrates Cuban culture and the achievements of Latin American artists. Among the celebrities who have earned stars on Calle Ocho are the rapper Pitbull and Selena, the late singer who is often described as the queen of Tejano music.

Getting Involved in Phoenix Politics

The head of the city government in Miami is Mayor Francis X. Suarez, the son of Cuban immigrants. Likewise, Reading's city government is headed by Mayor Eddie Morán, who was born in Puerto Rico. It would seem, then, that Latinos have made great strides in the political world—ascending to positions in which they can have a direct impact on the communities where they live. But that is not true in all places where Latinos have chosen to make their homes. A 2020 study by the news organization *USA Today* found that just 1 percent of US elected officials at the local, state, and federal levels are of Latino descent. Clearly, Latinos have found paths into elected office, but usually they are council members or legislators representing districts where a majority of voters are Latino. More significant offices—among them governorships and seats in the US Senate—have largely remained beyond the reach of many Latino political leaders.

Among the successful Latino political leaders is Carlos García, who won election to the city council in Phoenix, Arizona. An immigrant from Mexico, García arrived in the United States at the age of five. He was brought across the border by his mother illegally; later, García was granted legal status, and he eventually became a US citizen. García grew up in the Arizona city of Tucson, later moving to the state capital of Phoenix. In 2007, while living in Phoenix, he founded the organization Puente Human Rights Movement (in English, *Puente* means "Bridge") to help Latino immigrants find housing, food, and other basic needs after arriving in the city.

Phoenix has a significant Latino population. Of the city's 680,000 residents, 42 percent trace their roots to Latin American countries. In 2020, García ran for Phoenix City Council; aided in no small part by the Latino vote, he won the election.

As a city council member, García fought hard for the Latino community, often sparring openly with Phoenix's mayor, Kate Gallego, particularly over her plan to evict many poor people—mainly Latinos—from mobile homes parked illegally on private properties. Many of those properties were vacant lots whose owners

Carlos García is pictured speaking in Phoenix in 2017, in protest of a speech made by then-president Donald Trump. García is one of many successful Latino political leaders.

desired to construct homes, retail stores, and other commercial uses. "There should be no hesitation for us to protect you all and to protect these homes,"[31] García told mobile home residents at a public forum on the issue in 2023. But García's campaign to save the mobile home residents from eviction was ultimately defeated. The Phoenix City Council voted down his plan to protect the mobile home residents, and Gallego ordered the evictions.

Shortly afterward, García lost his election bid for another term on the council. For the foreseeable future, his advocacy for Latino immigrants will have to come from outside the chambers of government. Elvia Díaz, a columnist for the *Arizona Republic*, writes, "García's departure represents a turning point for the less fortunate who need champions like him on the council."[32]

Activists such as García have helped make communities like Phoenix more welcoming to Latino immigrants. Elsewhere, Latino immigrants have helped revive struggling American communities by opening new businesses and forging careers as doctors, lawyers, teachers, and others who serve as foundations for city life. Immigrants from Latin America have also enhanced the vibrant culture and texture of cities across America.

CHAPTER FIVE

Immigrants of Distinction

The United States has become home to many distinguished immigrants from the countries of Latin America. Their achievements can be seen in science, the arts, sports, technology, and business, among other areas. Desi Arnaz, who immigrated to the United States from Cuba during the 1930s, became one of America's most popular musicians, band leaders, comedians, and TV producers. Race car driver Daniel Suárez was born in Mexico; since 2013, he has starred on the NASCAR racing circuit in the United States. Mario Molina, who immigrated to the United States from Mexico in 1968, determined how air pollution eats away at the ozone layer—the portion of the upper atmosphere that protects life on Earth from harmful rays emitted by the sun. In 1995, Molina was awarded the Nobel Prize—the world's most esteemed award for science.

Their achievements, and the achievements of many other Latin American immigrants, have contributed to the fabric of American life. They have built on established traditions and helped to create new ones. Their achievements range across many facets of life, from developing innovations in the technology sector to stardom in Hollywood to exploring issues of importance to Americans through their talents in journalism.

Protecting People Online

People who sign on to online retailers as well as other websites often encounter an initial first step: they are asked by the site to retype a group of letters that are often presented on-screen in a distorted typeface. This program is known as CAPTCHA. It is used by websites to ensure that the user trying to gain access to the site is an actual human, not a bot that could help a scammer gain access to the user's account.

CAPTCHA was developed by Luis von Ahn, who immigrated to the United States from Guatemala in 1996 at the age of seventeen. Von Ahn had long been interested in technology. When he was a young boy, his mother bought him a Commodore 64 computer, which was one of the first computers sold to consumers for home use. Although the computer was obsolete by the time von Ahn could use it, it was the best computer his mother could find at the time. It whetted von Ahn's interest in technology and mathematics. As a senior in high school in Guatemala he was contacted by Duke University in Durham, North Carolina, and invited to submit an application to enroll. He was accepted, achieved his bachelor's degree in mathematics at Duke, and then enrolled in Carnegie Mellon University in Pittsburgh, where he worked toward a doctorate in computer science.

Daniel Suárez, pictured here at the Las Vegas Motor Speedway in 2019, was born in Mexico. He has starred on the NASCAR racing circuit since 2013.

> "Your brain was doing something that computers could not yet do. Computers could not recognize those distorted characters."[33]
>
> —CAPTCHA creator Luis von Ahn

In 2000, while studying at Carnegie Mellon, von Ahn developed CAPTCHA. At the time, von Ahn says, computer scientists were concerned about the ease with which websites could be hacked. Von Ahn says it was clear to him that the software employed by hackers to break into online accounts was incapable of unraveling a random set of letters. "Your brain was doing something that computers could not yet do," he says. "Computers could not recognize those distorted characters."[33]

After achieving his doctorate from Carnegie Mellon in 2005, von Ahn elected to stay in Pittsburgh, where he established a company that further developed and refined CAPTCHA. Later CAPTCHA versions included a series of photos users were asked to identify. Four years later, he sold the company to the California tech giant Google for several million dollars. He took his profits from the CAPTCHA sale and in 2011 founded a new company. That company, Duolingo, provides an app for smartphones and computers

Luis von Ahn, pictured here in 2007, is an immigrant from Guatemala. He has been very successful in the field of technology.

that helps users learn and understand foreign languages. What makes Duolingo unique is it gathers data from all users attempting to learn one of the forty languages available on the app. The software can tell what parts of the language—the words, phrases, usage, punctuation, and other elements—are most challenging for students. Armed with that information, the Duolingo software is constantly tailoring itself to simplify those problem areas, helping students achieve better skills in foreign languages.

Von Ahn developed Duolingo with Severin Hacker, a classmate from Carnegie Mellon. Hacker is an immigrant from Switzerland. Before leaving their home countries, both von Ahn and Hacker had learned to speak English. Von Ahn says English is a vital skill for immigrants who arrive in America and aspire to establish successful careers. "We decided that we wanted to teach languages because of English," says von Ahn. "We're both non-native English speakers. In both of our cases English changed our lives, and in most countries in the world, knowledge of English can significantly increase [immigrants'] income potential."[34]

By any measure, von Ahn—an immigrant from Guatemala—has forged an impressive career. He has helped protect the privacy of perhaps hundreds of millions of computer users while also offering a pathway for people to learn languages and thus enhance communication on a global scale.

Creating Gloria

Over the past two decades, Sofía Vergara has become one of America's most popular actresses. Known mostly for her role as Gloria on the hit TV comedy *Modern Family*, which ran for twelve seasons on the ABC network, Vergara has also appeared in many other TV shows and films. Starting in 2020, she has served as a judge on the hit TV variety show *America's Got Talent*. In 2023, she caused something of a storm when she angrily walked off the stage after bickering with a fellow judge, the comedian Howie Mandel. During the episode, Mandel had been playfully needling Vergara about her recent divorce from her husband, actor Joe

Desi Arnaz's Contributions to American Comedy

Desi Arnaz arrived in America in 1933. He emigrated from Cuba, which, at the time, was embroiled in revolution. He was a talented musician and eventually became a bandleader. But it was as a TV producer that Arnaz proved himself a cutting edge figure. Married to actress Lucille Ball, Arnaz and Ball produced one of the first situation comedies to air on American TV: *I Love Lucy*, which premiered in 1951.

Arnaz introduced some techniques to the production that are still employed by TV producers today. For example, Arnaz insisted that *I Love Lucy* be filmed in front of a live audience. Being able to respond to an audience improved the performances of the actors. "In the early 1950s, while the rest of Hollywood wondered whether television was more than a passing fad, Lucy and Desi were already breaking the rules, making great art, and building the future of broadcasting," says Laura LaPlaca, director of archives at the National Comedy Center, a museum in Jamestown, New York, that focuses on American comedy, "They were innovators behind-the-scenes, risk-takers in business, and masters of the comedic craft."

Quoted in Maureen Lee Linker, "Why Lucy and Ricky Are Still the Gold Standard for Television Couples," *Entertainment Weekly*, February 15, 2022. https://ew.com.

Manganiello. When Mandel asked Vergara whether she was in the market for a new boyfriend, Vergara snapped, "That's it!"[35] She then walked off the stage but returned a few minutes later to raucous applause from the audience. The whole playful episode illustrates how Vergara's popularity and her sense of humor helps drive the success of the show, which is watched by some 6 million viewers each week.

Born in 1972 in the Colombian city of Barranquilla, Vergara began working as a fashion model in her teens. Her popularity as a model soared in her home country. Soon after turning twenty, Vergara was offered a contract hosting a Colombian-produced TV show that focused on travel. The show, *Fuera de Serie* (in English, Out of the Ordinary), was also carried by American cable TV providers. Producers in America saw the show and offered Vergara hosting opportunities for Spanish-language shows created for cable TV in the United States. Vergara accepted the jobs but also started learning English with the desire to win roles on TV networks in America.

Vergara immigrated to the United States in 1998—but not because of her work on American TV. Rather, she decided to move after her brother Rafael was murdered in Colombia. Authorities suspected the killers originally intended to kidnap Rafael and hold him for ransom, which they felt Vergara could pay given her TV earnings. But their plan went violently awry, and Rafael lost his life. Vergara and her parents decided then that their home country was not safe, and so they moved to Miami.

Now an established actress in America, Vergara found herself fielding many offers from TV producers in the United States. In 2009, she was offered a role on *Modern Family*, a comedy that followed the antics of a supposedly typical American family. Vergara played Gloria, a vivacious Latin American immigrant who is the second wife of the family patriarch. Among the other characters were a father near retirement age, an uncle who is gay, a daughter who is a ditzy party girl, another daughter who is a nerdy genius, and a son who pursues his dream to become an actor. Vergara became a very popular member of the cast and believes her role helped introduce the life of a Latina immigrant to many American viewers. "I am grateful for the opportunity because the [TV producers] have let me in with this strong accent I have," she said as the show entered its ninth season. "Eight years ago nobody had an accent like this on television."[36]

> "Eight years ago nobody had an accent like this on television."[36]
>
> —Actress Sofía Vergara

In 2020, the show's producers elected to bring *Modern Family* to a close. Since the series concluded, Vergara has continued to appear in TV and film roles. In 2024 she took a step away from comedy when she starred in the Netflix drama series *Griselda*. Vergara plays the title character Griselda Blanco, the real-life head of a notorious crime syndicate. Meanwhile, she has also become an entrepreneur, launching a company that makes women's clothing; a production company that develops TV programming for Latino audiences; and Raze, an internet-based TV network that features Latino programming.

Vergara gives credit for her success to her character Gloria, and the fan base she created, for making it all possible. She says,

> I created Gloria as a mixture of my mom and my aunt and the women that I grew up with in Colombia—they were loud, they were super intense, they were super colorful, super crazy, minding everybody's business, super passionate and loving. If Gloria was a stereotypical woman, then what a magnificent stereotype. What was wrong with being Gloria? She was fantastic. She cared about everyone, she loved everyone . . . she was always trying to help everyone.[37]

Exploring the World as a Journalist

Lulu Garcia-Navarro is a familiar name in American broadcast journalism. She has spent more than twenty years reporting on some of the most important stories that have emerged across the world, often stepping into war zones to provide audiences with updates

An immigrant from Colombia, Sofia Vergara (sitting in the center of the photo) has become one of America's most popular actresses. In 2009, she was offered a role on the sitcom Modern Family, a comedy that followed the antics of a supposedly typical American family. Vergara played Gloria, a vivacious Latin American immigrant.

on the violent conflicts. Most recently, she has hosted the podcast *First Person*, which is produced by the *New York Times* newspaper.

For the podcast, Garcia-Navarro interviews people who are not well-known newsmakers. Rather, she looks for people who are attempting to make a difference behind the scenes, changing how others view the world or react to events unfolding around them. Among the guests she has interviewed are a Missouri college professor who is striving to draw young Black people into careers in law enforcement; a Tennessee doctor who is defying his state's ban on abortion to save women who are experiencing life-threatening pregnancies; a New York City teen who is leading a movement to convince other young people to give up their smartphones; and a Utah sheriff who trains teachers in the use of guns for protection against mass shooters.

In all her interviews, Garcia-Navarro says she strives to uncover facts that help people shape their views of the culture in which they live. "Journalism isn't just about writing things down or recording things or speaking in public," she says. "The core of journalism is being curious about the world, asking questions, and making sure that you get good answers. And the skills that you learn in journalism are applicable to so many different types of jobs. Journalism teaches you to dig deeper, to synthesize information in a way that people can understand and easily digest, and to communicate well."[38]

Prior to taking over the podcast in 2021, Garcia-Navarro spent seventeen years as a reporter for National Public Radio (NPR). During her career with NPR, she served as an international correspondent assigned to cover news events unfolding in other countries. During her tenure at NPR, she covered stories in Mexico, Cuba, Libya, and Syria.

Garcia-Navarro's parents married as teenagers in Cuba (her mother is of Panamanian descent), but soon after their wedding the couple fled the Caribbean nation. They moved first to London, where their daughter Lourdes—"Lulu" is her preferred nickname— was born in 1970. Later, the family moved to Miami, where Garcia-

Helping Entrepreneurs Launch Their Businesses

The US Small Business Administration (SBA) is a federal agency established to help entrepreneurs start new businesses ranging from corner delicatessens to tiny home remodeling businesses. The SBA provides assistance for small business owners on how to hire employees, how to navigate the nation's tax laws, and how to find bank loans to finance their enterprises. From 2014 to 2017, the SBA was headed by Maria Contreras-Sweet, an immigrant from Guadalajara, Mexico.

She arrived in America in 1960 at the age of five. Years later, she founded the California-based ProAmérica Bank, which focuses on providing loans to Latino immigrants to help them start their own businesses. As head of the SBA, she oversaw an agency that not only aided businesses owned by Latino immigrants but also by all Americans. In appointing Contreras-Sweet to head the SBA, President Barack Obama said,

> Maria . . . told me a wonderful story about how her grandmother, back in Mexico who was a migrant worker, said to her that if she worked hard, studied, stayed in school, that someday she'd be able to work in an office as a secretary and really make her proud. . . . And now she's going to be helping the folks who are following behind her achieve their dreams. That's what America is all about.

Quoted in Bill Chappell, "Obama Nominates Maria Contreras-Sweet to Head SBA," *The Two-Way* (blog), National Public Radio, January 15, 2014. www.npr.org.

Navarro spent her childhood and teen years. Garcia-Navarro first started considering a career in journalism while still in her teens. She says, "There was something in me even then that wanted to explore the world and understand it."[39]

Her first job in journalism was working as a freelance radio reporter for the British Broadcasting Corporation, the national broadcast network in Great Britain. She soon found full-time work with the news service Associated Press, most significantly covering the Iraq War during the early years of the 2000s. She joined NPR in 2009. In 2017 she became a US citizen. That was also the year she was named the Sunday anchor of *Weekend Edition*, a popular news analysis show on NPR. She says,

> "There was something in me even then that wanted to explore the world and understand it."[39]
>
> —Journalist Lulu Garcia-Navarro

What I'm most proud of is being the first Latina to host an NPR news program. It makes me sad that it only happened in 2017. I think that says something about the state of the journalism industry. But I'm proud that I have been able to raise the profile of the Latino community on a major news network and engage in conversations about how we use Spanish on the air, how we pronounce names, and what kind of stories we are elevating. These to me are essential questions. As a journalist working out in the world, I covered things that were really important. But they were about a moment in time. Being able to sit in a chair and address millions of people and try to elevate the stories of an entire community—to me, that is the most profound thing I've done so far.[40]

Von Ahn, Vergara, and Garcia-Navarro are among the many Latino immigrants who have risen to the top of their chosen professions. They arrived in America intent on not just settling in as productive members of their new homeland but also aspiring to be leaders and trendsetters—Latino immigrants of distinction who are serving as role models for others.

SOURCE NOTES

Introduction: An Immigrant's Path to Stardom

1. Quoted in Natalia Trejo, "Ana de Armas Talks Humble Upbringing in Cuba and Wearing Her Brother's Hand-Me-Downs," *Hola!*, February 7, 2020. www.hola.com.
2. Quoted in Parker Schug, "Lilimar: On Her Mission to Explore Her Passion for Performing and How Being a Young Actress Has Forced Her to Grow Mentally Stronger," *Grumpy*, March 1, 2019. https://grumpymagazine.com.

Chapter One: Arrivals

3. Quoted in Transnational Working Communities, "Interview with Rigoberto Garcia Perez," December 2, 2001. http://dbacon.igc.org.
4. Jia Lynn Yang, *One Mighty and Irresistible Tide: The Epic Struggle over American Immigration, 1924–1965*. New York: W.W. Norton, 2020, p. 251.
5. Quoted in Transnational Working Communities, "Interview with Rigoberto Garcia Perez."
6. Michele Cantos, ed., "The Latino Impact on Food Systems," *Hispanic Executive*, October 2, 2023. https://hispanicexecutive.com.
7. Mark Hugo Lopez and Mohamad Moslimani, "Most Latino Immigrants Say They Would Come to the US Again," Pew Research Center, January 20, 2022. www.pewresearch.org.
8. Quoted in Michael Hall, "He's One of the Best Young Prosecutors in Texas. He Also Could Get Kicked Out of the Country," *Texas Monthly*, December 19, 2019. www.texasmonthly.com.
9. Quoted in Hall, "He's One of the Best Young Prosecutors in Texas."

Chapter Two: Getting Work

10. Quoted in Jesse Thompson, "Family First: Three Hispanic and Latino Employees Share Their Stories," BlueCross BlueShield of Tennessee, October 6, 2021. https://bcbstnews.com.
11. Quoted in Thompson, "Family First."
12. Quoted in Samantha Roberts, "Immigrants Play Essential Role in Textile Industry," *Atlanta Journal-Constitution*, December 29, 2017. www.ajc.com.

13. Quoted in Roberts, "Immigrants Play Essential Role in Textile Industry."
14. Quoted in NBC News, "A Shifting Economic Landscape: U.S. Latinos Discuss Jobs, Income," March 18, 2015. www.nbcnews.com.
15. Quoted in Beatriz Paniego-Béjar, "Stories of Our Community: Latina Workers," *UnidosUS Blog*, June 9, 2022. https://unidosus.org.
16. Quoted in NBC News, "A Shifting Economic Landscape."
17. Quoted in NBC News, "A Shifting Economic Landscape."

Chapter Three: Creating New Businesses

18. Quoted in Lemelson Foundation, "From Plastic Surgeon-in-Training to Inventor: How a Family Tragedy Led One Latina to Improve Lung Disease Diagnosis for the World," February 8, 2022. www.lemelson.org.
19. Quoted in Lemelson Foundation, "From Plastic Surgeon-in-Training to Inventor."
20. Quoted in Dwight Torres, "The Immigrant Restaurant Owner from a Country Without Food," The Click, December 8, 2020. https://theclick.news.
21. Quoted in Torres, "The Immigrant Restaurant Owner from a Country Without Food."
22. Quoted in Torres, "The Immigrant Restaurant Owner from a Country Without Food."
23. Quoted in Institute for Immigration Research, "El Salvador: Summary of Interview with Carlos Castro," George Mason University, 2023. https://iir.gmu.edu.
24. Quoted in Institute for Immigration Research, "El Salvador."
25. Quoted in Institute for Immigration Research, "El Salvador."

Chapter Four: Helping to Build Vibrant Communities

26. Quoted in Seth Kugel, "Leaving New York, with Bodega in Tow," *New York Times*, October 29, 2006. www.nytimes.com.
27. Quoted in Jake Blumgart, "Did Latino Immigrants Save the American City?," *Governing*, June 16, 2022. www.governing.com.
28. Quoted in Blumgart, "Did Latino Immigrants Save the American City?"
29. Quoted in Associated Press, "Cubans Making Risky Boat Trip to Florida, Another Immigration Challenge for Biden Administration," CBC News, January 25, 2023. www.cbc.ca.
30. Generator, "Experience Cuban Culture in Miami." https://staygenerator.com.

31. Quoted in Christina Estes, "Phoenix Leaders Willing to Fight Developers to Save Mobile Home Parks," KJZZ, March 7, 2023. https://kjzz.org.
32. Elvia Díaz, "It Matters That Phoenix Councilman Carlos Garcia Fought the Mayor on His Way Out," *Arizona Republic*, April 19, 2023. https://www.azcentral.com.

Chapter Five: Immigrants of Distinction

33. Quoted in Nate Skid, "Meet the 43-Year-Old 'Genius' Behind $2.79 Billion Language App Duolingo," CNBC, January 25, 2023. www.cnbc.com.
34. Quoted in Em Nguyen and Amanda Su, "Meet Luis von Ahn, the Guatemalan Immigrant Behind the World's Most Popular Language App Duolingo," ABC News, November 16, 2022. https://abcnews.go.com.
35. Quoted in Kelly Martinez, "Why Sofía Vergara Said 'That's It!, and Walked Off *America's Got Talent*," *People*, September 14, 2023. https://people.com.
36. Quoted in Kate Dwyer, "Sofia Vergara: 'What's Wrong with Being a Stereotype?,'" *Time*, January 26, 2017. https://time.com.
37. Quoted in *Variety*, "Sofia Vergara: The Businesswoman Behind a Beloved Sitcom Star," May 6, 2021. www.nbcnews.com.
38. Quoted in Lindsay López-Isa Lamken, "Lulu Garcia-Navarro: On the Record with Lateenz!," Lateenz, April 6, 2022. https://lateenz.com.
39. Quoted in López-Isa Lamken, "Lulu Garcia-Navarro."
40. Quoted in López-Isa Lamken, "Lulu Garcia-Navarro."

FOR FURTHER RESEARCH

Books

Sherrie Baver, Angelo Falcón, and Gabriel Haslip-Viera, eds., *Latinos in New York: Communities in Transition*. Notre Dame, IN: University of Notre Dame Press, 2017.

Alberto García, *Abandoning Their Beloved Land: The Politics of Bracero Migration in Mexico*. Oakland, CA: University of California Press, 2023.

Juan Gonzalez, *Harvest of Empire: A History of Latinos in America*. New York: Penguin, 2022.

Bill Nowlin and Julio M. Rodriguez, eds., *Dominicans in the Major Leagues*. Phoenix: Society for American Baseball Research, 2022.

A.K. Sandoval-Strausz, *Barrio America: How Latino Immigrants Saved the American City*. New York: Basic Books, 2019.

Barbara Sheen, *The Dreamers and DACA*. San Diego: ReferencePoint, 2020.

Internet Sources

Jake Blumgart, "Did Latino Immigrants Save the American City?," *Governing*, June 16, 2022. www.governing.com.

Elvia Díaz, "It Matters That Phoenix Councilman Carlos Garcia Fought the Mayor on His Way Out," *Arizona Republic*, April 19, 2023. www.azcentral.com.

Michael Hall, "He's One of the Best Young Prosecutors in Texas. He Also Could Get Kicked Out of the Country," *Texas Monthly*, December 19, 2019. www.texasmonthly.com.

Lindsay López-Isa Lamken, "Lulu Garcia-Navarro: On the Record with Lateenz!," Lateenz, April 6, 2022. https://lateenz.com.

Variety, "Sofia Vergara: The Businesswoman Behind a Beloved Sitcom Star," May 6, 2021. www.nbcnews.com.

Websites

Centro Hispano of Reading and Berks County
www.centrohispano.org
Among its services, this organization helps residents of the Pennsylvania city find health care and apply to colleges, and it teaches new parents techniques for caring for their children. By accessing the "Legal" tab on the group's website, visitors can find the Centro Hispano study, which traces the demographic evolution of Reading into a community with a majority Latino population.

Immigration Legal Resource Center (ILRC)
www.ilrc.org
The ILRC advocates for legal status for undocumented immigrants. By accessing the "DACA" link on the ILRC website, visitors can find resources for migrants who wish to apply for protection under the DACA program as well as updates on the numerous legal cases that have been filed to make the program permanent.

Transnational Working Communities: Braceros & Border Jumpers
http://dbacon.igc.org/TWC/b0_Index.htm
This organization records the histories of immigration waves to the United States, and its website focuses on the plight of the braceros. Visitors to the website can access interviews with several former braceros, including Rigoberto Garcia Perez, as well as others from Latin America who tell their stories of migration to the United States.

UnidosUS
https://unidosus.org
Based in Washington, DC, this group aids low-income Latino immigrants and advocates for their rights. By accessing the "Blog" link on the organization's website, visitors can find the stories of many Latino immigrants and the struggles and successes they have experienced in establishing homes and careers in their adopted country.

US Citizen and Immigration Services
www.uscis.gov/green-card
This federal agency's website provides information on the permanent residence card, known as a green card. By accessing the link for "Green Card Eligibility Categories," students can explore the many reasons migrants come to the United States, including educational opportunities, reunions with family members, and protection from criminals in their home countries.

INDEX

Note: Boldface page numbers indicate illustrations.

Aghion, Alberto, 35
Almanzar, Ana Palmira, 26–27
Arnaz, Desi, 46, 50
Artunduaga, Maria, 28–30

Ball, Lucille, 50
Barroso, Diana, 19–20
Blonde (film), 7, **7**
border crossings, illegal, 15–16
Bracero Program, 9, 11–13, **12**, 17
Bureau of Labor Statistics, US, 25
businesses, created by immigrants
　in construction, 33–34
　in food/groceries, 32–33, 34
　in health care, 28–30
　numbers of, 30–31
　pet care, 31
　in technology, 46–49
　Zumba classes, 35

Cambrón, María, 21, 24
Cantos, Michele, 14
CAPTCHA program, 46–48
Castillo, Miguel Angel Navarro, 31–33
Castro, Carlos, 33–36
Census Bureau, US, 41, 43
　on apprehensions of illegal border crossers, 15
Center for American Progress, 17, 22

Centro Hispano of Reading and Berks County, 60
Chang-Díaz, Franklin, 8
chronic obstructive pulmonary disease (COPD), 28
Citizenship and Immigration Services, US, 16, 60 [ED: "Citizen" here]
college degrees, percentage of Latino immigrants earning, 20
Contreras-Sweet, Maria, 54
COVID-19 pandemic, 22
Cuba, 6
Customs and Border Protection, US, 15

de Armas, Ana, 6–7, **7**
Deferred Action for Childhood Arrivals (DACA), 16
de la Renta, Oscar, 8
del Toro, Guillermo, 13
Department of Agriculture, US, 13
Department of Labor, US, 20
　on average earnings of housekeepers, 25
　on average earnings of restaurant servers, 24
Díaz, Elvia, 45
Diaz, Jeiler del Toro, 42
Dolejs, Richard, 40
Dominican Republic, 26
Dreamers, 15–16
　contribution to American society by, 17–18
Duolingo (app), 48–49

61

farm laborers, **12**
   Bracero Program and, 12–14
Feliz, Yessy, 31
First Person (podcast), 53
Food and Drug Administration, US (FDA), 30
food trucks, 30–33, **32**

Gallego, Kate, 44
García, Carlos, 44–45, **45**
Garcia-Navarro, Lulu, 52–55
Garcia Perez, Rigoberto, 9–10, 13
Griselda (drama series), 51

health care field
   businesses created by immigrants in, 28–30
   granting legal status to immigrants would benefit, 17
Hernandez, Lilimar, 8

I Love Lucy (TV program), 49
immigrants, in US
   statistics on, **4–5**
   unemployment rate among, 20
Immigration Legal Resource Center (ILRC), 60
El Internado (Spanish TV series), 7

Jawetz, Tom, 22

LaPlaca, Laura, 50
Latinas, employment as housekeepers, 24–26
Latino immigrants
   beneficial impacts on big cities from, 40–41
   future in STEM fields, 25
   during Mexican Revolution, 10
   numbers holding jobs as essential workers during COVID-19 pandemic, 22
   numbers of/countries of origin, 15
   percentage earning college degrees in US, 20
   percentage employed in US service sector, 23
   as percentage of foreign-born workforce in US, 20
   percentage of US businesses owned by, 31
   percentage working in manual labor, 20–21
   as political leaders, 44–45
   reasons for immigrating, 14
Little Havana, 41–43, **42**

Mexican immigrants
   Bracero Program and, 12–14
   US labor force and need for, 10–11
Mexican Revolution (1910–1920), **11**
Migration Policy Institute, 20, 23
Modern Family (TV program), 49, 51
   cast of, **52**
Molina, Mario, 46
Moore, Margaret, 17–18
Morán, Eddie, 44

National Comedy Center (Jamestown, NY), 50
National Institutes of Health, 28

Obama, Barack, 16, 54

Pennsylvania Dutch community, 37

Perez, Beto, 35
pet-sitting services, 31
Pew Research Center, 14, 15–16
  on percentage of Latino immigrants earning college degrees, 20
Pitbull, 43

quinceañera celebrations, 40

Ramírez, Jorge, 21–22
Reading, PA, 37–38, 40, 44
Rojas, Yolanda, 43
Roque, Miriam Paredo, 25–26

Sanchez, Aquiles, 23–24
Sandoval-Strausz, A.K., 41
secondary migration, 38
Selena, 43
Small Business Administration, US (SBA), 54
Stanford University, 31
Suárez, Daniel, 46, **47**
Suarez, Francis X., 44

Transnational Working Communities: Braceros & Border Jumpers, 60

undocumented immigrants, 16
unemployment rate, for foreign vs. native-born Americans, 20
UnidosUS, 25, 60
United States
  Latino immigrants as vital to economy of, 17
  Latino share of total foreign-born workforce in, 20
  population born in Latin American countries, 15
  statistics on immigration in, **4–5**
USA Today (newspaper), 44

Vergara, Sofía, 49–52, **52**, 55
Villalobos, Pedro, 16–18
von Ahn, Luis, 47–49, **48**, 55

War Dogs (film), 7
Watford City, ND, 43
Wilkie, Chris, 25

Yang, Jia Lynn, 10–11

Zarzuela, Gregorio, 39
Zumba, 35

PICTURE CREDITS

Cover: Shutterstock.com

4: Shutterstock.com
5: Shutterstock.com
7: Netflix/Photofest
11: Hum Images/Alamy Stock Photo
12: Associated Press
15: Norma Jean Gargasz/Alamy Stock Photo
21: pixelheadphoto digitalskillet/Shutterstock.com
23: BearFotos/Shutterstock.com
27: Jeffrey Isaac Greenber 4+/Alamy Stock Photo
30: MBI/Alamy Stock Photo
32: Jeffrey Isaac Greenberg 18+/Alamy Stock Photo
34: David Grossman/Alamy Stock Photo
39: H. Mark Weidman Photography/Alamy Stock Photo
42: F1online digitale Bildagentur GmbH/Alamy Stock Photo
45: Associated Press
47: Grindstone Media Group/Shutterstock.com
48: Associated Press
52: ABC/Photofest

Charts and Graphs by Maury Aaseng

Sources: Immigrants in the United States (pages 4–5)
- Shannon Schumacher, et al, "Understanding the U.S. Immigrant Experience: The 2023 KFF/LA Times Survey of Immigrants," Sep 17, 2023. www.kff.org.
- Joel Rose, "The Immigrant Population in the U.S. Is Climbing Again, Setting a Record Last Year," September 14, 2023. www.npr.org.
- "Immigrants in the U.S. Economy: Overcoming Hurdles, Yet Still Facing Barriers," Immigration Research Initiative, May 1, 2023. https://immresearch.org.
- Stuart Anderson, "Highly Skilled Immigrants Drive U.S. Innovation, Report Shows," *Forbes*, January 12, 2023. www.forbes.com.
- Shannon Schumacher, et al, "Understanding the U.S. Immigrant Experience: The 2023 KFF/LA Times Survey of Immigrants," Sep 17, 2023. www.kff.org.
- Yasmin Amer, "Immigrants Are 80% More Likely to Start Businesses in the U.S. than Native-Born Citizens, Study Finds," WBUR, May 09, 2022. https://www.wbur.org.
- "Citizenship and Immigration Statuses of the U.S. Foreign-Born Population," Congressional Research Service, October 19, 2023. https://sgp.fas.org/crs/homesec/IF11806.pdf.